Staten Island, New York 10312

STUNT DOGS

BY JANE MERSKY LEDER

EDITED BY DR. HOWARD SCHROEDER
Professor in Reading and Language Arts
Dept. of Elementary Education
Mankato State University

PRODUCED & DESIGNED BY
BAKER STREET PRODUCTIONS

CRESTWOOD HOUSE

LIBRARY OF CONGRESS CATALOGING IN PUBLICATION DATA

Leder, Jane Mersky.
  Stunt dogs.

  (Working dogs)
  1. Dogs in moving-pictures--Juvenile literature. 2. Dogs in television--Juvenile literature. I. Schroeder, Howard. II. Baker Street Productions. III. Title
PN1995.9.A5L48   1985   636.7'088   85-19469
ISBN 0-89686-289-5 (lib. bdg.)

International Standard
Book Number:
Library Binding 0-89686-289-5

Library of Congress
Catalog Card Number:
85-19469

ILLUSTRATION CREDITS

Alan Leder: Cover, 29, 30, 33, 34, 36, 39, 41, 45, 46
RCA: 5
AP/Wide World Photos: 8, 20, 22, 23, 27
UPI/Bettmann News Photos: 7, 11, 12-13, 15, 19, 24-25
Circus World Museum Photo: 42-43

Copyright© 1985 by Crestwood House, Inc. All rights reserved. No part of this book may be reproduced in any form without written permission from the publisher, except for brief passages included in a review. Printed in the United States of America.

CRESTWOOD HOUSE

Hwy. 66 South, Box 3427
Mankato, MN 56002-3427

Table of contents

Chapter I: Introduction 4
   Some famous stunt dogs
   Nipper: The RCA dog
   Rin Tin Tin
   Asta
   Lassie
   Dog stars today
   Benji

Chapter II: The making of a stunt dog 26
   Special qualities are needed
   Basic training rules
   Treats
   Praise
   Corrections
   Hand signals

Chapter III: Beginning-stunt training 34
   "Come"
   "Sit"
   "Stay"
   "Down"

Chapter IV: Advanced stunt training 40
   Natural-action stunts
   Giving a kiss
   Scratching
   Performance stunts
   Conclusion

Glossary: 47

1.
Some famous stunt dogs

You often hear the saying, "Dogs are a man's best friend." Dogs and people have been friends for at least thousands of years! Long ago, people relied on dogs to warn them of danger. In turn, dogs relied on people for food and shelter. As time passed, dogs became pets. They lived in their master's home. They played with the children. And they learned to do many important jobs.

Today, dogs perform a variety of jobs. Some dogs guide the blind. Others herd, or round up, animals like sheep and cows. Still others guard homes and businesses. And some very special dogs learn to do tricks and become stunt dogs. You see these dog "stars" in magazines and on television. You also see them in circuses and in the movies.

Nipper: The RCA dog

Some of the most famous dog stars went to work long before you were born. A fox terrier named Nipper won the love of Americans more than eighty years ago. That is when he first appeared in a magazine ad for an RCA

Victrola. (A Victrola is an early phonograph. Sounds come from a horn instead of from speakers.) In the ad, Nipper sat and listened to his master's voice coming from the horn of a Victrola. He was very cute and people could not easily forget him. Every time they thought about Nipper, they also thought of an RCA Victrola. Nipper helped sell thousands of Victrolas and other RCA products.

In 1968, RCA stopped using Nipper in its ads. The people at RCA thought it was time to try something new. A few years later, they changed their minds and brought Nipper back. Today Nipper is the symbol for RCA's ColorTrak TV sets.

Nipper listens to his master's voice.

Rin Tin Tin

Lee Duncan was selling sporting goods when World War I broke out. He quickly joined the Army Air Corps as a pilot. After training, Duncan was sent to France to fight. On September 13, 1918, he was told to inspect an airport that had been captured by the Americans. While poking around, he heard whining noises. He followed the sound. The sound led him to a trench about ten feet from the main airport building. A German shepherd and her six puppies were in the hole. The dogs shivered in the damp and cold weather.

Duncan quickly got towels and dried off the pups and their mother. He then took the family back to a nearby American base. When the pups were old enough, four of them were adopted by other soldiers. One male and one female were left. Duncan decided to keep the last two for himself. He named the male Rin Tin Tin and the female Nanette.

After serving his time in France, Duncan returned home with the two young dogs. Sadly, Nanette died just three days after reaching America. But Rin Tin Tin grew up to be a healthy, handsome dog. Duncan decided to enter Rin Tin Tin in a dog show. One of the judges said the dog was "clumsy." That made Duncan angry. He vowed to train Rin Tin Tin to be a champion.

Duncan used patience and love to train Rin Tin Tin. Soon, the dog could perform many stunts. One thing led to another, and in 1923, Rin Tin Tin appeared in

Rin Tin Tin gets ready for a 1931 "interview" on NBC radio.

A 1929 photograph that was signed by Lee Duncan.

his first movie. It was an adventure film, with no sound, called *Where The North Begins*. The public loved Rin Tin Tin from his first silent bark!

Over the years, Rin Tin Tin starred in nine movies. His last film was released in 1931. A year later, at the age of fourteen, he died. After his death, Rin Tin Tin, Jr., his "son" carried on the famous name in movies for several more years. But by 1938, it looked like the public had lost interest in Rin Tin Tin. There were no offers for new films. So for the next few years, Duncan raised horses, cattle, and German shepherds.

In early 1947, Duncan wanted to make a movie with Rin Tin Tin III. But there had not been a Rin Tin Tin film for many years. To see if there was interest in such a film, Duncan had a survey made to see if people remembered Rin Tin Tin. The results were amazing! Over seventy percent of the people interviewed knew the name Rin Tin Tin. Of this group, ninety-five percent said that they would like to see the dog in another film.

The Return of Rin Tin Tin was made soon after. It was the story of a young man who found love and happiness, with the help of a priest and a friendly German shepherd. The movie was very popular, but no other Rin Tin Tin movies were made.

Little was seen or heard of Rin Tin Tin for the next few years. Then television came into the homes of many Americans in the 1950's. Suddenly there was a demand for children's adventure shows. A television producer remembered how popular Rin Tin Tin films had been.

He got in touch with Lee Duncan about an idea he had. "Why not make Rin Tin Tin into a television show," he asked? Duncan loved the idea.

The Adventures of Rin Tin Tin went on the ABC Network on October 15, 1954. The show stayed on the air for almost five years. Even after ABC cancelled the show, it could be seen in reruns around the country for many years. During the 1960's, the show faded away. Rin Tin Tin and Lee Duncan finally retired for good.

Asta

One of the most popular film series from the 1930's and 1940's was called the *Thin Man* series. It starred William Powell, Myrna Loy, and a little wire-haired terrier named Asta. Asta's real name was Skippy. His job was to be cute, funny, and to help his masters uncover clues in murder cases.

Every *Thin Man* movie began with a murder. The police would arrive and proceed to bungle the investigation. Then Asta and his owners would find the murderer and tell the police how they solved the crime.

Over the years, several dogs played the role of Asta. They all looked alike. Fans thought the same dog was in all six of the movies that were made.

In 1941, a radio series based on the *Thin Man* went on the air. It was so much like the film series that most listeners thought the film stars played the radio parts. They were wrong. Unknown dogs and actors played the parts for almost ten years.

Skippy, the first Asta, receives an award from a human movie star, Humphrey Bogart.

Asta, as he looked in a 1938 movie, "The Awful Truth."

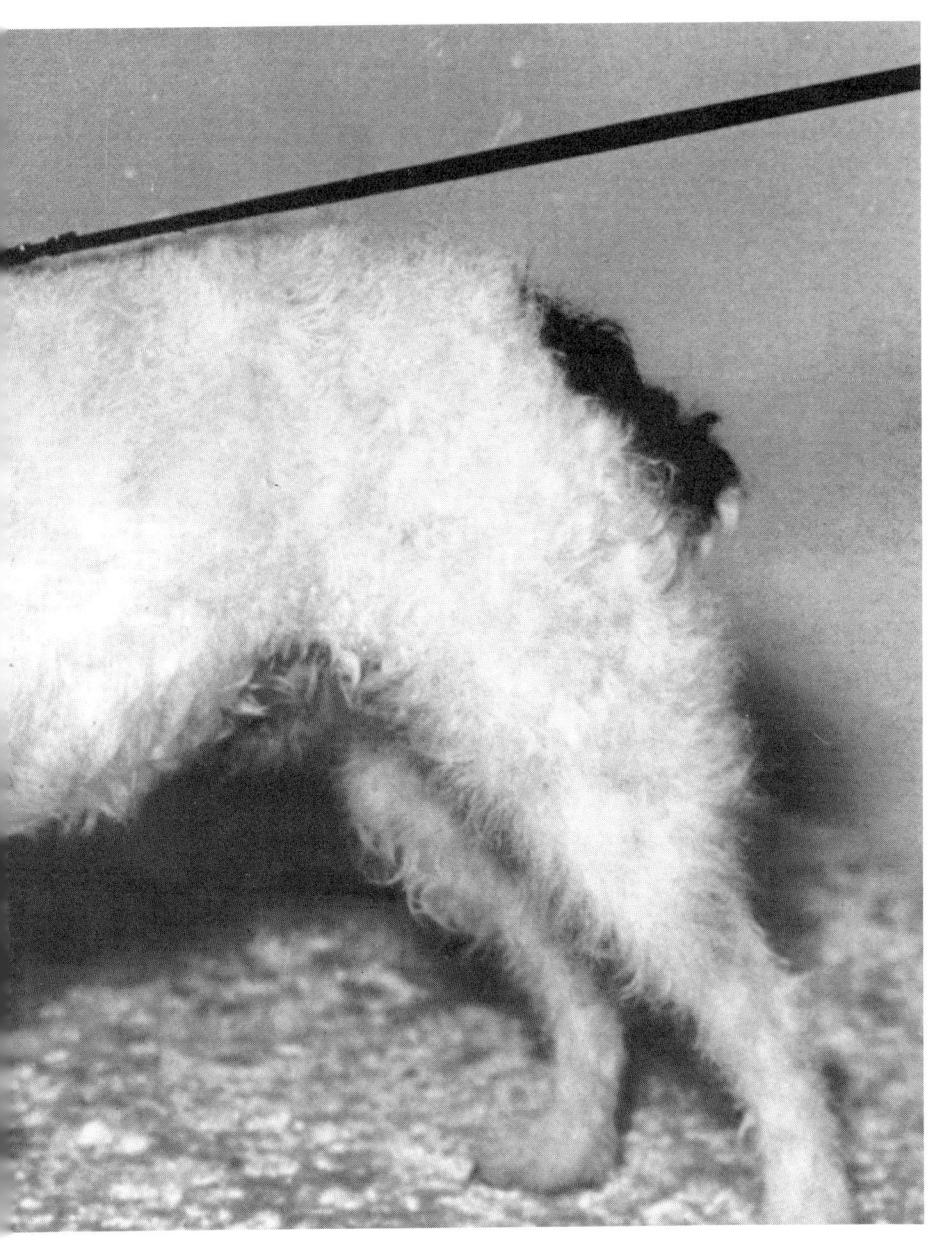

From the end of the radio series in 1950 until 1957, nothing was done with Asta or the *Thin Man*. But in 1957, the *Thin Man* was made into a television series. It starred Peter Lawford, Phyllis Kirk, and a wire-haired terrier whose real name was Asta. The program won many awards. Fans all over the United States were thrilled to see Asta and his friends for several more years.

At least three trainers worked with the different Astas over the years. They included Henry East, Frank Inn, and Rudd Weatherwax. Myrna Loy, one of the original *Thin Man* stars, talked about Weatherwax and Asta in an interview. "We couldn't be friendly with Asta," she said. "He was a trained dog and he had to respond to his master. Weatherwax was his master at the time. He was a wonderful man and was very good to his animals."

Loy went on to talk about how she got Asta to do tricks while they were filming. "He did everything for a little squeaky mouse," she said. "I'd squeak the mouse and put it in my pocket, and then Asta would do whatever he was supposed to do. He thought he was going to get the mouse. He never got the mouse. He'd get a cracker or something. Asta was a wonderful dog."

Lassie

Rudd Weatherwax, the man who trained Asta, also trained the best-known stunt dog in the world. His name was Lassie.

Lassie, the best-known stunt dog in the world.

In 1940, Weatherwax and his brother opened a dog school and kennel. (A kennel is a place where dogs are raised, trained, and boarded.) Soon after the kennel opened, a man brought in an eight-month-old collie named Pal. Pal was driving the man crazy. He barked all the time and chased cars. Weatherwax worked hard with Pal. He taught him not to bark so often, nor to chase cars. When Weatherwax called Pal's owner to pick the dog up, the owner said he did not want Pal any longer. He asked if Weatherwax would keep the dog in place of the seventy-five dollar training bill. Weatherwax immediately agreed. He thought Pal was a natural for the movies.

In 1941, the MGM film studio tried out over one thousand dogs to play the role of Lassie in a movie called *Lassie, Come Home*. Pal was one of the thousand dogs turned down for the role. MGM wanted a female. Pal was a male. However, Pal did get the job as the "double" to the animal chosen for the part. (A double is an actor who takes the place of a star if they're sick or hurt.)

For some reason that no one knows, the director of the film decided to use Pal in one scene. Pal had to swim across a river in California. The director felt that all wet Collies looked alike. The audience, he felt, would not be able to tell the difference between Pal and the real Lassie.

Pal swam the river. Then he climbed out on the bank with his tail between his legs and dropped right in front of the camera. He put his head between his paws and slowly closed his eyes. Weatherwax had Pal so well trained that he did not even shake when he came out of the river. That would have ruined the scene. The dog was suppose to be so tired that he could barely breathe.

The director was amazed. Pal played the scene better than he thought possible. Pal was given the role of Lassie on the spot. That is how his long career started.

Lassie, Come Home was a hit. It was the story of a young boy and his Collie. Because the boy's family was so poor, the dog was sold. There was not enough food to feed him. Lassie's new owner took the dog hundreds of miles away. But Lassie still loved the boy. He ran away and began the long trip home. On the way home, he faced many dangers. Finally, Lassie returned home to be with his former master.

Pal, now known as Lassie, made six more films for MGM. He earned millions of dollars for the studio and a quarter of a million dollars for Weatherwax. In 1951, MGM decided not to make any more Lassie films. Two years passed. Weatherwax began to fear that there was no future for Lassie. Then one day in 1953, a television producer met with Weatherwax. They talked about a television series for Lassie. Weatherwax liked the idea.

A test program was soon ready. Everyone loved the story about a farm boy, his dog, his friends and family. Over the next eighteen years, the television show, *Lassie*, was seen by millions of people every Sunday night.

Even though it has been out of production for many years, *Lassie* can be found at some time of the day or night on just about any television set in the world! Rudd Weatherwax sums up Lassie this way: "Pretty good for a dog that chased cars and wasn't wanted, eh?"

Dog stars today

Dogs are just as popular today as they were when Rin Tin Tin, Asta, and Lassie first became stars. Stunt dogs are used more than ever in television commercials and magazine ads. Sandy, the dog from *Annie*, has been used by Burger King. Ralph, a golden retriever, works for Magnavox. A Basset hound named Norman does commercials for Sony. But the dog who has become the best-known star of television commercials is Alex.

Alex was a stray dog who was "discovered" by a Hollywood agent. In his first commercial for Stroh's beer, four men are playing cards. One of them asks for a beer. Alex is sent to the kitchen to get it. The camera does not follow Alex to the kitchen. It shows the looks on the men's faces. They hear the sounds of a refrigerator door opening, bottles being opened, and beer being poured. Then they hear the sound of Alex drinking. Alex's owner shouts, "Alex, you better be drinking your water!" He is hoping Alex is not drinking the beer.

The commercial with Alex became very popular. It was very funny. Alex was a star.

Benji

The owners of a small film company in Dallas, Texas had a dream. They wanted to make a film that families could watch together. They also wanted to make the film in Texas. The experts said it could not be done. They were wrong.

Benji became a star that the whole family enjoyed.

Benji posed for a joke photograph in 1980, reminding people to get their income tax returns filed by April 15.

Joe Camp, the president of the film company, wrote the story himself. It was about a boy and girl who are kidnapped, then rescued by a dog. The movie was to be called *Benji*.

Joe Camp looked all over for the right dog to play Benji. He talked to dog trainers across the country. One trainer he met with was Frank Inn. Inn owned a mutt named Higgins. Higgins was part cocker, poodle, and Schnauzer. He had just retired from the television show called *Petticoat Junction*.

When Camp saw Higgins, he said, "He's the one."

"You don't want him," said Inn. "He's thirteen or fourteen years old!"

Nothing could change Camp's mind. He finally got Inn to let Higgins play the role of Benji.

"Joe told me what he wanted to do," said Inn. "I told him it was impossible. Then we went to work!"

Benji is a story told from the dog's point of view. The audience sees everything as if it were a dog. That caused some interesting problems. All camera equipment is made to film from a "people-point-of-view." So the equipment had to be remade. To fit Higgins' point of view, for example, the camera lens had to stand only a few inches off the ground!

Benji was a hit and Higgins received many awards. He was named "Animal Act of the Year for 1976." He also won a place in the American Humane Association's Hall of Fame. The only other dog to be named to the Hall of Fame was Lassie.

21

By 1978, *Benji* and the next film, *For The Love of Benji*, had made over sixty-five million dollars. Higgins was now a dog super-star. He even appeared on televi-

Unlike other dogs, Benji traveled in a regular seat on airplanes.

sion shows. A study that measures the popularity of stars listed Benji, a dog, right along with John Wayne, Bob Hope, and Carol Burnett!

Gary Coleman and Benji at the 1979, Emmy Awards.

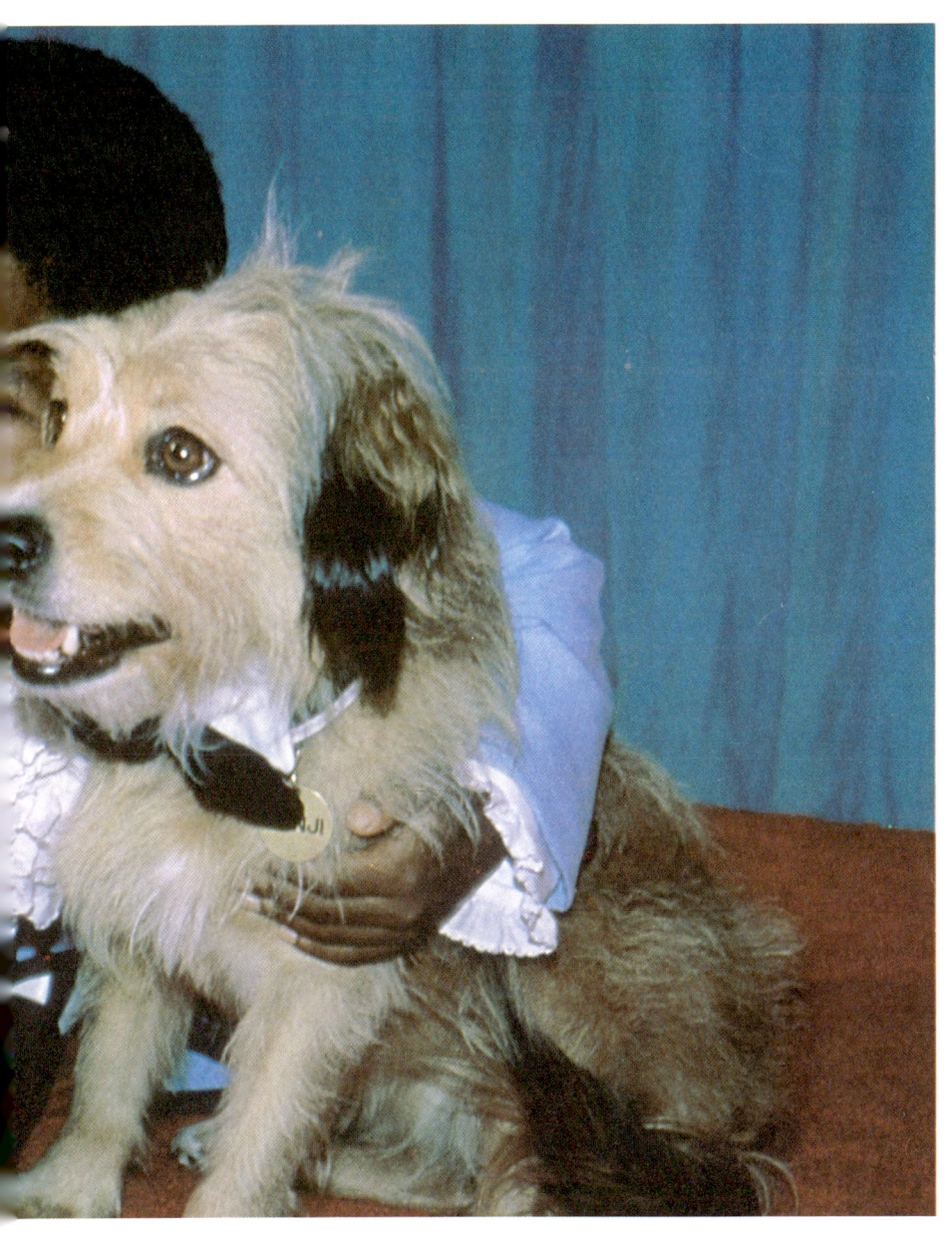

2.
Special qualities are needed

There are some forty-nine million pet dogs in America. Like Higgins, most of them are mutts. (A mutt is a dog whose parents are each different breeds, or types of dog.) The experts say that mutts have the best chance of becoming dog stars. They have what one dog agent calls a "mid-America look." Mutts look like the dog next door. Or almost. A mutt does not suggest meanness, like German shepherds. A mutt does not suggest wealth like a poodle. Mutts have broad appeal. That is the reason advertisers and film studios often prefer them.

Just any dog does not become a dog star, however. Most dog stars have a special look. They are unusual. Many people think they are adorable. Dog stars need to photograph well, and they have to enjoy working in front of a camera.

Dog stars must also like working with people. They must have a strong need to please. The best dog stars like to learn stunts. They enjoy the challenge of new tricks. Bob Hoffmann, a trainer in Chicago, said,

Dog stars like Sandy, who worked in the Broadway show, "Annie," must love to work with people.

"There is a look in the dog's eyes. It says, 'I'm a bright dog. Teach me something new.'"

A good stunt dog is happy to be trained and likes to perform. It is up to the trainer to see that the dog stays happy. No dog performs well when it is unhappy. If its tail is down and its head hanging, the trainer is not doing a good job.

Basic training rules

Some trainers like to train two or three times a day for fairly long periods. Others like ten to fifteen short training sessions spread over an entire day. No matter what the schedule, training must be interesting. The dog has to be pushed to learn, but it can't be pushed too far. Training is like a game. To be successful, it must be fun. The dog should look forward to training sessions.

A good trainer never gets angry at a dog. If he does, the dog knows it. Then the dog gets upset, too. Learning stops. Neither the dog nor the trainer can pay attention. If this happens the training has to stop for a time. Once the dog and trainer have had a chance to relax, they can start work again.

Dogs are not as sharp right after they eat. Therefore, it is best to train a dog before it has been fed. The dog will be more interested in food treats if it has not just eaten. The time after training is the time to treat the dog right. The dog needs to know that each session will

A trainer knows that dogs need affection.

end with love and treats. Many trainers play with their dogs and then walk them. In this way, the dog gets the affection it needs.

Trainers usually end a training session with the same word each time. This lets the dog know that a session is over. Most trainers say "O.K." But any word will do as long as the same word is used everytime. Many stunts require the dog to stay in one position until the trainer says its time to come out of it. Letting a dog out of a position is called "releasing" the dog. The word used to release the dog is called a release word. The same release word is used all the time.

Dogs get love and treats when a training session is finished.

Treats

Treats are an important part of stunt training. They should be small and taste great. Some trainers use little pieces of hot dogs. Others use cooked liver, chicken, or anything the dog really loves. The one treat rarely used is dog bones. Dog bones take too long to eat. They can also get caught in the dog's throat and make him cough. And dogs will not be interested in dog bones after the first or second treat.

Training treats are used only for training. They are not given to the dog at any other time. This keeps the treats special. Treats make training something for the dog to look forward to.

Praise

Praise is the main key to dog training. It is praise that makes the dog want to do its tricks. The more it is told how good it is, the harder it will try to please its trainer.

It does not really matter what words a trainer chooses for praising. Most trainers say "good dog" or "what a good dog." The most important part of praising is tone of voice. The trainer has to sound enthusiastic. If the trainer uses the right tone of voice, the dog will enjoy the praise and continue to work hard.

If the trainer is bored and does not really mean what he says, the dog will usually know it.

Corrections

When a dog is learning new stunts, there are always times when it must be corrected. Corrections show a dog what it is doing wrong. They are not a punishment. There is never a need to hurt the dog.

One correction often used involves snapping the dog's leash. The leash is attached to a collar around the dog's neck. When the leash is snapped, the collar tightens and gets the dog's attention. The sudden snap surprises the dog. It "wakes it up." It tells the dog it is doing something wrong.

Once a dog starts to do what is asked, it is tested without the correction. If the dog performs the trick correctly, it is rewarded and praised. If the dog stops obeying a command, the trainer corrects it again. A good stunt dog soon learns the trick and no longer needs a correction.

Hand signals

Stunt dogs, that appear in movies and commercials, need to learn hand signals. By using hand signals, a trainer can show the dog what to do without making a sound. Imagine you are watching the film *Benji*. Every time Benji does something, you hear his trainer giving a command. "Sit, Benji." "Lie down, Benji." "Push the door, Benji." Hearing the trainer talk would ruin the movie. That's why hand signals are important.

Dog trainer, Bob Hoffmann, teaches hand signals as soon as the dog knows what a word command means. Other trainers teach word commands and hand signals at the same time. Interestingly, a dog usually learns hand signals faster than word commands.

Most hand signals show a stunt dog what to do. The hand signal that tells a dog to "stay" looks like a policeman stopping traffic. The trainer pushes his hand, palm out, straight toward the dog. The dog will stay in one place until the trainer releases it.

To hand signal a dog to "lie down," the trainer moves his right hand, palm down, straight to the floor in front of him. This signal shows the dog the direction to go.

If a dog learns basic hand signals from the beginning of his training, it is much easier to teach more difficult stunt signals later.

Trainer, Bob Hoffmann, gives a hand signal for his dog to "stay."

3.
"Come"

Before any stunt work can begin, the trainer must be able to get the dog's attention whenever he wants it. That may sound simple. But imagine how silly the trainer would feel trying to show off a new stunt and having his dog ignore him. Let's follow Bob Hoffman as he trains a young, male dog named Sam. The

Trainer, Sandy Hoffmann, gives the hand signal to "lie down."

"Come" command teaches a dog to come close and pay attention. This stunt also helps build good feelings between the trainer and dog. The dog learns that coming close is always a nice experience.

To teach the "Come" command, the dog is walked around on a leash. When the dog starts to walk away, the trainer says, "Come." He snaps the leash. Then he pulls the dog toward him by moving his hands down the leash. When the dog is close, the trainer praises and pets him.

The same steps are done over and over. Between training sessions, the dog is walked around. This walk gives the dog time to relax.

Once the dog starts to come on command, before the snap of the leash, he is ready to be tested. If the dog comes after just hearing "Come," he is given lots of praise. Then the trainer walks the dog and tests him a few more times. When the dog comes on command several times in a row, it has learned the stunt.

"Sit"

Unless the dog sits when he is called, he will just stand around and look silly. Since dogs know how to sit, the trainer's job is half done. All he needs to do is teach the dog to sit when told.

To teach a dog to sit, the trainer first walks his dog on a leash. After a short walk, the trainer shortens the

The dog is hand signaled to "sit."

leash in his right hand. This is done by folding the leash. Now the trainer's hand is about a foot away from the dog. With his left hand, the trainer squeezes gently on the dog's haunches. (Haunches are a dog's hip, buttock, and upper thigh.) As the trainer squeezes, he says "Sit." As soon as the dog sits, the trainer gives lots of praise. Then he pulls up on the leash ever so slightly. This pressure keeps the dog sitting until the trainer starts to walk him again.

Once the dog begins to sit before the squeeze, it is time to try testing him with just a command. If the dog does not sit, the trainer goes back and repeats the steps again. When the dog sits without the squeeze several times in a row, he has learned the command.

"Stay"

There are different ways to teach a dog to stay in one place. One way is to say, "Stay," and then put the left hand in front of the dog's face. The palm of the hand should almost touch the dog's nose. If the dog starts to move, the trainer taps the dog on the nose. If this is done correctly, the dog will think that he, not the trainer, caused the tap.

Next, the trainer moves a few feet away from the dog. He stays away for a few seconds, and then returns. When he praises the dog, the dog thinks it has done something good.

The trainer then moves a little further away and stays a little longer. Then he returns and praises the dog. These steps are repeated several more times. The dog begins to learn that everytime the trainer leaves, he will return with praise.

If the dog leaves its place, the trainer corrects it. He takes the leash in both hands and bounces the dog back to its place. Then he leaves the dog again. Most trainers use this correction only once or twice. If the dog still does not stay, the trainer goes through the lesson again from the beginning.

"Down"

The "Down" command is quite simple. But for some strange reason, many dogs do not like it. A dog often gets tired and lies down. But when it is told to lie down, it will often refuse. Teaching a dog to lie down takes a lot of patience.

There are different ways to teach the "Down" command. One way to begin is to kneel next to the dog. Then place one hand on the dog's back and the other behind the lower part of its front legs. As the trainer says "Down," he pushes down on the dog's back and carefully pulls its legs out from under. As soon as the dog is lying down, it is praised.

After the dog is praised, it is pushed back into a sitting position. Then the steps are repeated over and over until the dog lies down with only a slight push on the back.

By now the dog has some idea of what the "Down" command means. It is ready for the next step. The trainer gets the dog in a sitting position. Then the trainer faces the dog and hooks his left thumb under the dog's collar. He turns his right hand palm down. By moving his hand straight down to the floor, the trainer shows the dog where he should go. Next, the trainer gives the command "Down" and pulls down on the dog's collar. Once the dog is down, the trainer removes his thumb from the collar, gives the "Stay" command, and praises the dog.

These steps are done over and over with less and less pressure on the collar. The big test comes when the trainer gives the command once. If the dog lies down, the training is a success.

Sandy Hoffmann pushes her dog into a down position.

4.
Natural-action stunts

Dogs need to be obedience-trained before learning more difficult stunts. That means they should be able to come, sit, stay, and lie down on command. If they do not know these commands, they will have a hard time learning anything else.

There are two basic kinds of dog stunts. There is the kind like "Stay," where the dog learns a new action. These are called performance stunts. And there is the kind like "Sit," where the dog does something it can do naturally. These are called natural-action stunts. Kissing and scratching are advanced natural-action stunts. Dogs do these things often. The trick is to get them to act on command.

Natural-action stunts are all taught the same way. First, the trainer gets the dog to do what he wants. While the dog does it, the trainer says the command and praises the dog. The trainer might also reward the dog with a treat for more difficult stunts.

Giving a kiss

For this stunt the trainer needs some tasty, sticky liquid. Honey is the best choice, but syrup, molasses,

A big wet kiss!

or gravy can also be used. The trainer smears the tasty liquid all over his face. Then he bends down toward the dog. When the dog starts licking, the trainer says "Kiss" or "Wash my face" and praises the dog. It is important to praise while the dog is licking. That way, the dog will learn what is being asked of him.

In the beginning, both the trainer and dog get pretty sticky! After a few times, the amount of liquid can be cut down. Eventually, the dog is tested without the sticky liquid. Once he does the trick several times in a row, there is no need to use the sticky liquid. Praise will be enough of a reward.

Jumping rope is an advanced performance stunt.

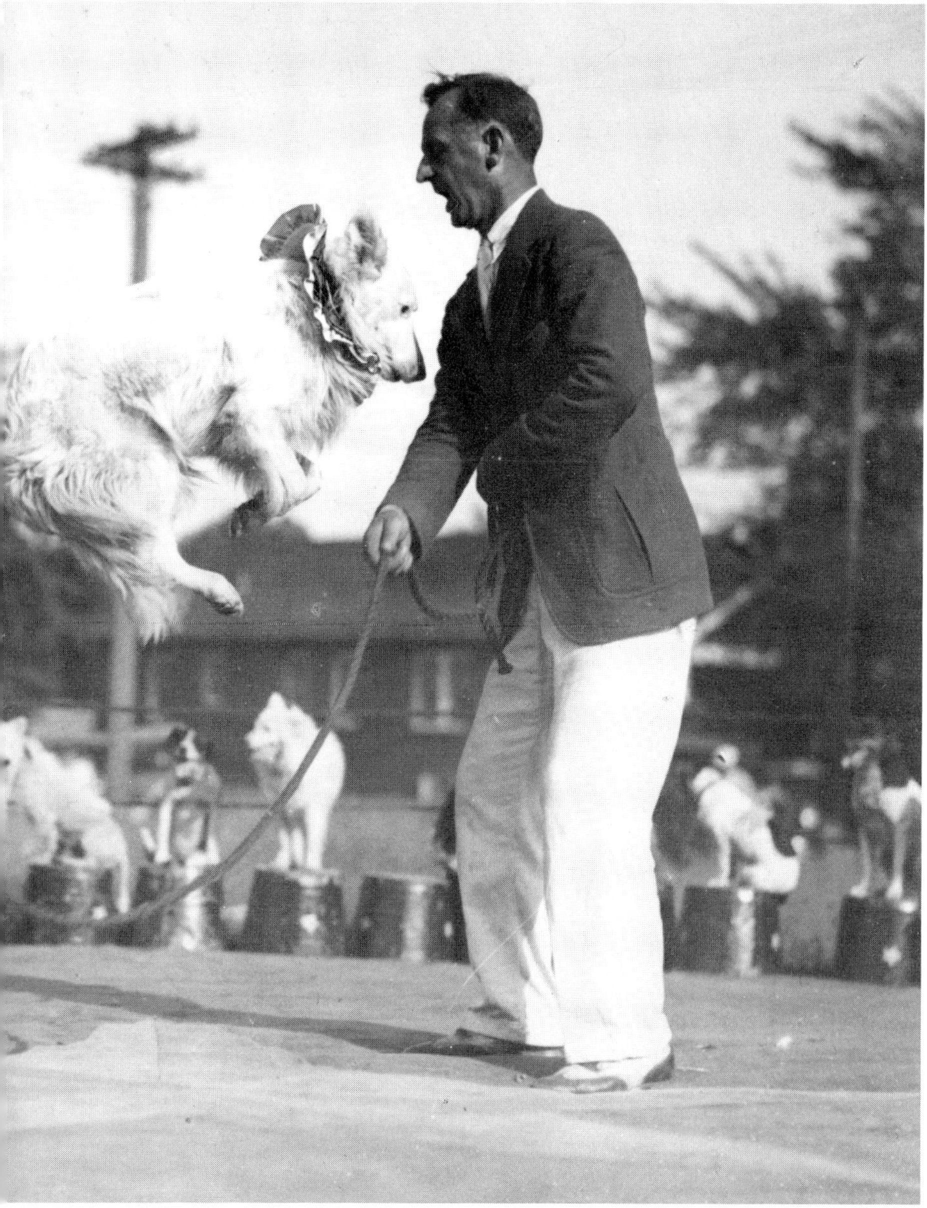

Scratching

Mr. Lucky, a dog trainer, says the easiest way to get a dog to scratch is to use a small clothespin. He suggests attaching the clothespin to loose skin on the dog. When the clothespin is put on the skin, the dog scratches. If the trainer says "Scratch," and then rewards the dog often enough, the dog will soon scratch on command without the clothespin.

Performance stunts

Advanced performance stunts are the hardest tricks to teach a dog. You will never see a dog naturally shake hands or say his prayers. Yet dog stars perform these and other stunts.

When a dog says his prayers, he looks very serious. But he will probably make the audience laugh. On command, the dog will kneel down. Then he will put his head between his paws just like he is saying his prayers. Even the meanest dog looks sweet when he does this trick.

Sometimes a trainer may get a call asking for his dog to appear in a television commercial. The people who write the commercial send the trainer a storyboard. A storyboard shows step-by-step drawings of how the commercial will be filmed. The trainer looks at the drawings. He sees what the dog will have to do. Sometimes the dog already knows many of the tricks. Sometimes the dog must learn several new ones.

Good stunt dogs love to perform!

Conclusion

Stunt dogs can do almost anything. Or so it seems. They leap fences, open bolted doors, shake hands, and even take bows.

Learning to perform these tricks takes a lot of time and hard work. The dog must want to learn something new. The trainer must have the patience to go over and over the same steps.

Dog stars are like actors and actresses in many ways. They learn parts. They work under hot camera lights. They often work long hours with little rest. And, of course, they lap up all the attention. Dog stars seem to know when the lights are on and the cameras are rolling. They love being in the spotlight!

Bosco is trained to surprise circus audiences by popping out of a box.

Glossary

"COME" COMMAND — *Command that teaches a dog to come close to the trainer and pay attention.*

"DOWN" COMMAND — *Command that teaches a dog to lie down.*

HAUNCHES — *A dog's hip, buttocks, and upper thighs.*

HAND SIGNALS — *Hand motions used in place of word commands that show a dog what to do.*

KENNEL — *A place where dogs are raised, trained, and boarded.*

MUTT — *A dog whose parents are of different breeds, or types.*

NATURAL-ACTION STUNT — *A stunt based on something a dog does naturally, like yawning or stretching.*

OBEDIENCE TRAINING — *Teaching a dog to sit, stay, come, and lie down.*

PERFORMANCE STUNT — *A stunt that is not based on a natural action.*

PRAISE — *Words from a trainer telling a dog how good he is; the key to dog training.*

RELEASE WORD — *A word used to let a dog out of a position.*

"SIT" COMMAND — *Command that teaches a dog to sit when told.*

"STAY" COMMAND — *Command that teaches a dog to remain in one place until released.*

STORYBOARD — *A series of drawings that show what a television commercial will look like.*

TREAT — *Food given to a dog after he does something correctly during training.*

VICTROLA — *An early phonograph with a horn instead of speakers.*

WORKING DOGS

READ ABOUT THE MANY KINDS OF DOGS THAT WORK FOR A LIVING:

- **HEARING-EAR DOGS**
- **GUIDE DOGS**
- **WATCH/GUARD DOGS**
- **LAW ENFORCEMENT DOGS**
- **SEARCH & RESCUE DOGS**
- **STUNT DOGS**
- **SLED DOGS**
- **MILITARY DOGS**

CRESTWOOD HOUSE